THIS COLORING BOOK BELONGS TO:

_____

This coloring book is dedicated to the Black equestrians before me. Your legacy lives on.

For the children I have met and will meet. I hope they never forget me or my horse, GOAT.

ISBN-13: 978-1-7361948-0-5
Black Equestrian Coloring Book Volume One: The Trailblazers
Copyright © 2020 by Caitlin Gooch
All rights reserved. This book or parts thereof may not be reproduced in any form, stored in any retrieval system, or transmitted in any form by any means—electronic, mechanical, photocopy, recording, or otherwise—without prior written permission of the publisher, except as provided by United States of America copyright law.

For permission requests, please contact the author via the "Contact" page on the following website: www.bygooch.com

Color and Learn
Black Equestrian Coloring Book
Volume One: The Trailblazers

CREATED BY CAITLIN A. GOOCH

ILLUSTRATED BY WHIMSICAL DESIGNS BY CJ

Cover Design
Sue M. Thompson

Additional Art
Kayla Dennis

Bass Reeves
1838-1910

Bass Reeves was a Deputy U.S. Marshal. He caught outlaws (criminals) and served justice on horseback. He was feared, respected, and strong. He arrested over 3,000 outlaws.

CATHY WILLIAMS
1844-1891

Cathy Williams was the first documented woman to enlist in the United States Army. She wanted nothing more than to provide for her family and friends and saw the army as a way to earn money for them. Unfortunately, when she was seventeen, she was separated from her mother by the Union army and forced to work as military support.

On July 28, 1866 congress passed the Act to Increase and Fix the Military Peace Establishment of the United States. This allowed Black men to enlist in the US army. However, in order for her to enlist, she had to disguise herself as a man.

Robert Lemmons

1848-1947

Robert "Bob" Lemmons rode his black horse, Warrior, to track down herds of wild mustangs. He was accepted into the herds after days of following them, and he learned a lot about wild horses by observing them. He acted like he was a mustang to make the horses think he was one of them. This is how he was able to takeover herds so they would follow

Nat Love
1854-1921

Nat Love was born on a slave plantation in Tennessee. At fifteen years old, he left his family and headed west. A cattle drive was coming through Dodge City, Kansas when he saw a few Black cowboys. He asked the boss for a job. To get the job he had to ride a horse named Good Eye. It was the worst ride Nat Love ever had, but he stayed on and got the job. He was paid $30 per month as a cowboy. He was also an expert roper and rider.

Isaac Burns Murphy

1861-1886

Isaac Burns Murphy was a Black jockey. He was known for being honest and loyal. He is the first jockey to win two Kentucky Derbys in a row, and he won 40% of his races despite negativity and corruption in the industry. He owned horses and trained horses for other people.

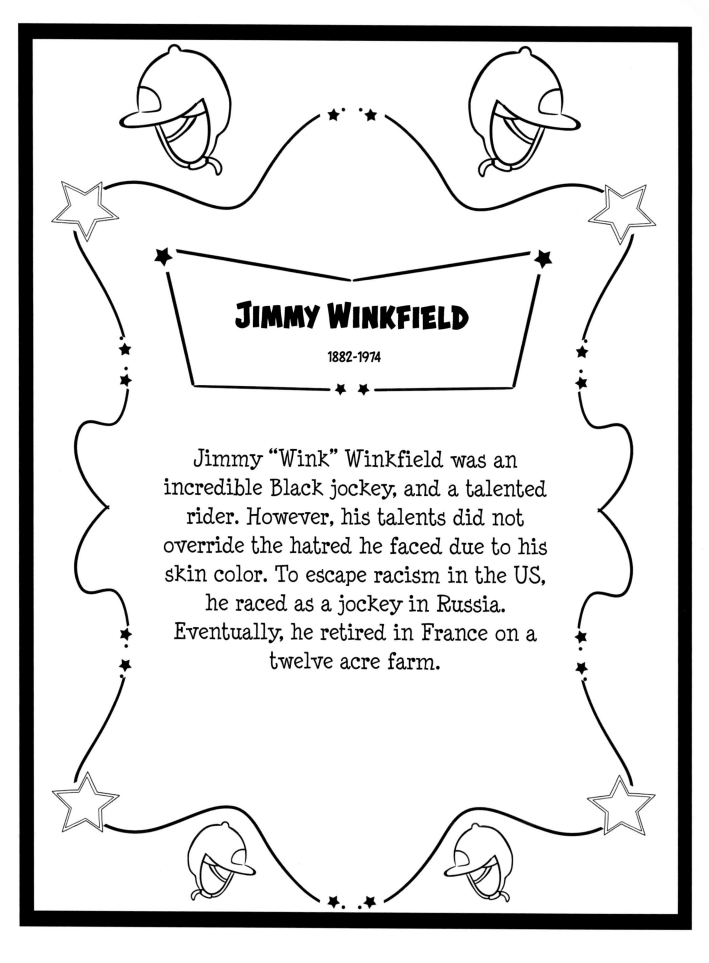

Jimmy Winkfield

1882-1974

Jimmy "Wink" Winkfield was an incredible Black jockey, and a talented rider. However, his talents did not override the hatred he faced due to his skin color. To escape racism in the US, he raced as a jockey in Russia. Eventually, he retired in France on a twelve acre farm.

George Fletcher

1890-1973

At a young age, George Fletcher played by pretending to ride broncos, and he grew up to become a bronc rider. George competed in the 1911 Saddle Bronc Championship. He was cheated out of his victory, but was a crowd favorite. He rode his best no matter what people thought of his skin color.

Sylvia Bishop
1921-2005

Sylvia Bishop loved horses. Raised in Charles Town, West Virginia, her love for horses started at the race track. In her teenage years she learned how to groom horses and ride. Soon after, she began to exercise horses on the race track. She is the first Black woman in the United States to become licensed to train thoroughbreds.

Cheryl White
1953-2019

Cheryl White was the first Black woman jockey in United States history. In her career as a jockey, she won 750 races. She raced against men at tracks all over the US. She even won two races on the same day in different states.

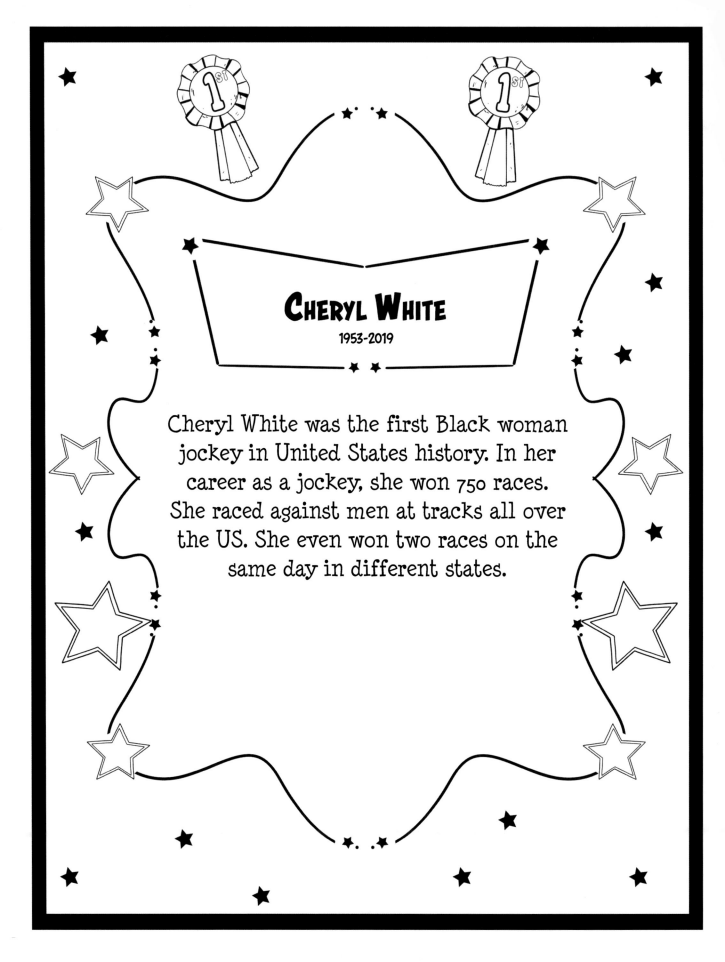

Black Beauty Queens

Although fairs and beauty contests were segregated at the time, Black people were still able to host their own. Oftentimes during parades at Black fairs, pageant winners rode on floats pulled by horses.

EQUESTRIAN

An equestrian is someone who rides or performs on horseback. Trail riders, jockeys, cowboys, cowgirls, bronc riders, western riders, english riders, bareback riders, etc., are equestrians.

You are the next generation of equestrians.

PHOTO BY TK FARRIER

DRAW YOURSELF AS AN EQUESTRIAN

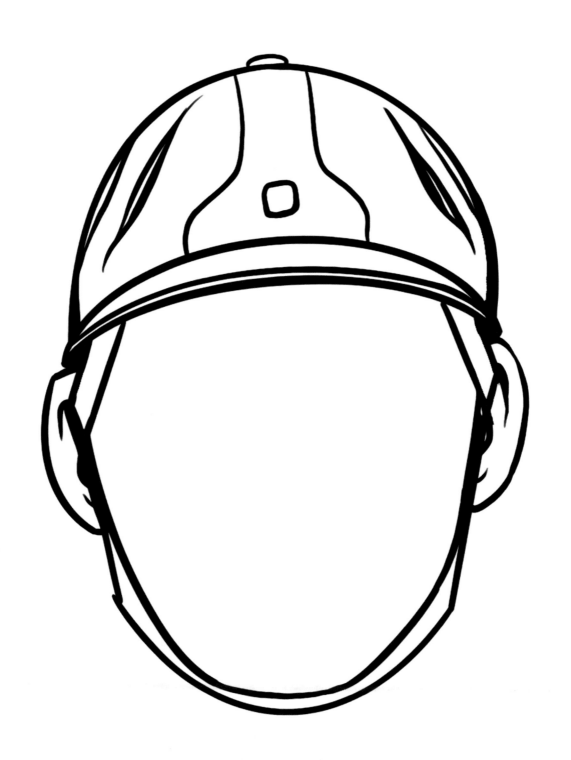

DRAW YOURSELF AS AN EQUESTRIAN

Made in the USA
Middletown, DE
13 November 2021